I0797779

101 PRAYERS FOR MY *Daughter*

ROB AND JOANNA TEIGEN

Christian Art
PUBLISHERS

Visit Christian Art Gifts, Inc., at www.christianartgifts.com.

101 Prayers for My Daughter

© 2016 by Rob and Joanna Teigen. Redesigned and reformatted 2024.
All rights reserved.

Published by Christian Art Gifts, Inc., Bloomingdale, IL, USA.

First edition 2024.

Designed by Christian Art Gifts, Inc.

Cover and interior images used under license from Shutterstock.com.

Scripture quotations are taken from the *Holy Bible*,
New International Version® NIV®. Copyright © 1973, 1978, 1984, 2011
by International Bible Society. Used by permission of Biblica, Inc.®
All rights reserved worldwide.

© All rights reserved. No part of this book may be reproduced in any form without permission in writing from the publisher, except in the case of brief quotations embodied in critical articles or reviews.

ISBN 978-1-63952-760-1

Printed in China.

29 28 27 26 25 24
10 9 8 7 6 5 4 3 2 1

Printed in Shenzhen, China
September 2024
Print Run: PUR404650

Children are a heritage
from the Lord, offspring
a reward from Him.

Psalm 127:3

01

Assurance of Salvation

Jesus said to her, "I am the resurrection and the life. The one who believes in Me will live, even though they die; and whoever lives by believing in Me will never die. Do you believe this?"

JOHN 11:25-26

LORD GOD,

I pray that my daughter would believe in Jesus with all of her heart. Open her eyes to see that life is found through faith in You alone. Let my precious child become Your child, as well. Give us the hope of eternity spent together with You—and each other—as we put our trust in You. Amen.

02

Friends for Life

Two are better than one, because they have a good return for their labor: If either of them falls down, one can help the other up. But pity anyone who falls and has no one to help them up.

ECCLESIASTES 4:9-10

LORD,

My daughter needs a friend. It's painful to feel left out and alone. When hard days come, there's no one to care and offer an encouraging word. Give her someone to stay by her side and help her up when she falls down. Let her experience Your faithful love through the joy of a true friend that loves her, too. Amen.

. 03

Peaceful Rest

In peace I will lie down and sleep, for You
alone, LORD, make me dwell in safety.

PSALM 4:8

FATHER GOD,

My daughter is struggling to sleep. Stress and worry make peaceful rest impossible. Pour out the gift of sweet sleep that will refresh her body and spirit. Quiet her anxious thoughts and agitation. Keep Your faithful watch over my child, so she can find perfect peace and rest in Your loving care. Amen.

04

A Humble Heart

Do nothing out of selfish ambition or vain conceit. Rather, in humility value others above yourselves, not looking to your own interests but each of you to the interests of the others.

PHILIPPIANS 2:3-4

LORD GOD,

You've blessed my daughter with intelligence, talent, and creativity. Keep her from using these gifts to seek praise and attention for herself. Give her a humble heart that can celebrate the achievements of others. Help her to recognize that her strengths come from You, in order to make her a blessing. Be glorified as she lifts others up and serves in Your name. Amen.

05

Patience in Everything

My dear brothers and sisters, take note of this:
Everyone should be quick to listen, slow to speak and
slow to become angry, because human anger does
not produce the righteousness that God desires.
JAMES 1:19-20

FATHER,
My daughter lashes out when she's angry, without considering how she might hurt other people. Teach her to listen and think before she responds to the frustrations that come her way. Give her patience to bear with others' weaknesses. Humble her heart to gracefully receive correction. Set her free from the trap of a quick temper, so she can grow in Your righteousness. Amen.

06

Her Prayer Life

In the morning, Lord, You hear my voice; in the morning I lay my requests before You and wait expectantly.

PSALM 5:3

LORD,

Teach my daughter to pray. Let her seek You every morning of her life. Help her to place every problem in Your hands. Give her faith to believe You will hear and answer. Set her free from fear and doubt that will keep her far from You. Respond to her prayers with Your loving power—You will do more than she can ask or imagine. Amen.

07

Healing Touch

Heal me, Lord, and I will be healed; save me and
I will be saved, for You are the one I praise.
JEREMIAH 17:14

FATHER,
When my daughter is sick and weary, restore her strength and encourage her spirit. Save her from doubting Your goodness and power. Teach her to rest in You, believing You are in control. Give her endurance to bear the pain. May Your perfect work of healing bring praise to Your name. Amen.

08

The Truth of God

Love does not delight in evil but rejoices with the truth.

1 CORINTHIANS 13:6

LORD GOD,

I pray that my daughter would live in Your truth. Renew her mind by Your perfect Word. Fill her mouth with honest words that glorify You. Keep her heart free from deception and secrecy. Give her integrity to keep her promises and admit her mistakes. Protect her from the confusion of false teaching. Let her love You more and more as she finds You always faithful and true. Amen.

09

Modesty & Goodness

I also want the women to dress modestly, with decency and propriety, adorning themselves, not with elaborate hairstyles or gold or pearls or expensive clothes, but with good deeds, appropriate for women who profess to worship God.

1 TIMOTHY 2:9-10

FATHER GOD,

Let my daughter's beauty come from a spirit of humility, generosity, and love. Guard her heart from craving attention through fashion and sex appeal. Give her courage to submit to Your will and Your ways, even if she doesn't fit in with the crowd. May her modesty and goodness be an act of worship as she devotes herself to You in everything she does. Amen.

10

Obedience & Instruction

Children, obey your parents in the Lord, for this is right. "Honor your father and mother"—which is the first commandment with a promise—"so that it may go well with you and that you may enjoy long life on the earth."

EPHESIANS 6:1-3

O LORD,

Open the door to blessing for my daughter as she learns to obey. Give her a humble heart that can submit to my instructions. Make her teachable, avoiding pain and trouble by following my direction. Give her an honoring attitude, and make me worthy of her respect. May she obey me out of love for You, for Your name's sake. Amen.

11

Contentment & Gratitude

You desire but do not have, so you kill. You covet but you cannot get what you want, so you quarrel and fight. You do not have because you do not ask God.

JAMES 4:2

LORD,

Guard my daughter's heart from jealousy. Fill her with gratitude instead of craving the blessings of others. Let her bring every desire to You in prayer instead of fighting for what she wants. Give her patience to wait for every good thing You have in store for her. Thank You for lavishing Your love on my daughter—may she praise Your name! Amen.

12

A Life of Peace

"Blessed are the peacemakers,
for they will be called children of God."
MATTHEW 5:9

FATHER,

Let my daughter pursue peace with everyone. Give her humility to admit when she's wrong and the strength to make amends. Help her to forgive when she's offended, seeking reconciliation instead of revenge. Restore her relationships as she learns patience, compassion, and love by Your Spirit. Amen.

13

A Godly Life

His divine power has given us everything we need for a godly life through our knowledge of Him who called us by His own glory and goodness.

2 PETER 1:3

LORD GOD,

I pray that my daughter would live in obedience to You. Fill her mind with an ever-growing knowledge of You and Your Word. Strengthen her by Your power to accomplish every purpose and plan You've created for her life. Let her righteousness and goodness shine as a light in this dark world. May she bring glory to Your name as she lives for You. Amen.

14

Happiness & Joy

May the righteous be glad and rejoice before God; may they be happy and joyful.

PSALM 68:3

FATHER,

Fill my daughter with happiness and joy. Open her eyes to see Your gifts and her heart to rejoice in Your love. Give her a cheerful spirit that is grateful in every situation, trusting that You are with her. Use her positive attitude to encourage others when they're feeling down. Be her greatest delight—knowing You is better than any pleasure this world can hold. Amen.

15

Her Self-Worth

You created my inmost being; You knit me together in my mother's womb. I praise You because I am fearfully and wonderfully made; Your works are wonderful, I know that full well.

PSALM 139:13-14

LORD JESUS,

Thank You for creating my beautiful daughter. You planned every detail of her personality, her intellect, and her appearance. Give her faith to believe she is a wonderful, incredible work of God Himself. May she be convinced of her important place in this world—that she is destined by You, cherished by me, and loved through and through by her heavenly Father. Amen.

16

Comfort from Above

The Lord is close to the brokenhearted and saves those who are crushed in spirit.

PSALM 34:18

FATHER,

Draw near to my daughter in times of difficulty. Let her rest in You and bring all her troubles to You. Where sadness and doubt consume her thoughts, bring peace and faith that You're in control. Where she is tired and discouraged, renew her strength and hope for tomorrow. Thank You for holding my daughter in Your arms. Amen.

17

Diligence in All She Does

Whatever you do, work at it with all your heart, as working for the Lord, not for human masters, since you know that you will receive an inheritance from the Lord as a reward. It is the Lord Christ you are serving.

COLOSSIANS 3:23-24

LORD GOD,

Give my daughter the strength to accomplish all that is before her today. Fill her with courage when the work seems too difficult. Help her persevere to the end, leaning on You when she's tired or discouraged. Capture her heart with a desire to serve You above anyone else. Let her receive Your wonderful rewards for her diligence and obedience today. Amen.

18

An Unshakable Faith

Without faith it is impossible to please God, because anyone who comes to Him must believe that He exists and that He rewards those who earnestly seek Him.

HEBREWS 11:6

LORD,

Fill my daughter's heart with an insatiable longing for You. May she seek You earnestly and discover the rewards You have in store. When the world denies Your Word and rejects Jesus, give her strength to hold on to the truth. Replace her doubts with assurance, and her confusion with clarity. Be pleased with my daughter as she grows in faith and trust. Amen.

19

Her Treasure

"Store up for yourselves treasures in heaven, where moths and vermin do not destroy, and where thieves do not break in and steal. For where your treasure is, there your heart will be also."
MATTHEW 6:20-21

FATHER,
Guard my daughter's heart from the love of money. May she place her hope in You, trusting in Your faithfulness to meet every need. Let her live to build Your kingdom instead of her bank account. Give her a spirit of gratitude and generosity so she can share Your blessings with others. Keep her eyes fixed on You—expectantly waiting for eternity with You in heaven. Amen.

20

Freedom from Pride

Live in harmony with one another. Do not be proud, but be willing to associate with people of low position. Do not be conceited.

ROMANS 12:16

FATHER,

Teach my daughter to be a true friend. Keep her from pride and selfishness that strives for popularity. Give her a loving heart that reaches out to others, regardless of how they fit in with the crowd. Use her as a peacemaker so that no one is left out or rejected. May her kindness and compassion shine the light of Jesus wherever she goes. Amen.

21

Worship & Praise

I rejoiced with those who said to me,
"Let us go to the house of the Lord."
PSALM 122:1

LORD GOD,

I pray that my daughter would love Your church. Give her joy as she gathers with other believers to worship. Let her experience Your presence as the Word is preached and praises are lifted up in prayer and singing. Envelop her in love through the ministry of Your people. Use the church to build her faith and knowledge of You. Amen.

22

Bless Her Future Marriage

"'For this reason a man will leave his father and mother and be united to his wife, and the two will become one flesh.' So they are no longer two, but one flesh. Therefore what God has joined together, let no one separate."

MARK 10:7-9

FATHER,

Even now, prepare my daughter and her future husband for their life together. Build them up in faith so they can live in obedience to You. Give them an unshakable commitment to each other that will stand the test of time. When disappointments, troubles, and temptations come their way, let them lean on You and hold fast to one another. Give them unity by Your Spirit that can never be broken. Amen.

23

Spiritual Protection

Be alert and of sober mind. Your enemy the devil prowls around like a roaring lion looking for someone to devour. Resist him, standing firm in the faith, because you know that the family of believers throughout the world is undergoing the same kind of sufferings.

1 PETER 5:8-9

LORD GOD,

Guard my daughter from the enemy—he wants to make her suffer and destroy her life. Give her discernment to detect his lies and schemes. Fill her with courage to resist him, believing Your Word and trusting in Your love. May she flee temptation, live in Your truth, and stand firm in the faith without wavering. Surround her with believers so she doesn't have to face the enemy alone. Amen.

24

Repentance & Forgiveness

Whoever conceals their sins does not prosper, but the one who confesses and renounces them finds mercy.

PROVERBS 28:13

HOLY FATHER,

Humble my daughter's heart to admit whenever she makes a mistake. Fill her with godly sorrow that will keep her from rest until she's confessed her sin to You. Help her to trust in Your mercy and promises to forgive. Let her commit her way to You, turning from the path of sin and back to obedience. Bring her healing and joy as she gives herself fully to You. Amen.

25

Her Worries

"Why do you worry about clothes? See how the flowers of the field grow. They do not labor or spin. Yet I tell you that not even Solomon in all his splendor was dressed like one of these."

MATTHEW 6:28-29

LORD JESUS,

Guard my daughter's heart from worry about clothes. She longs for acceptance and could place hope in her appearance instead of You. Set her free from the pressure to keep up and fit in with the world's definition of beauty. Give her contentment and a thankful heart for what You've provided in her closet. Let her trust You to meet her needs since You care for every detail of her life. Amen.

26

Friends in Faith

I do not sit with the deceitful, nor do I associate with hypocrites. I abhor the assembly of evildoers and refuse to sit with the wicked.

PSALM 26:4-5

FATHER,

Give my daughter wisdom in choosing her friends. Open her eyes to discern those who live out their faith from their heart instead of just empty religion. Keep her from joining in with gossip or competing for popularity. Give her a gentle, kind spirit to keep her from taking part in bullying, or excluding or slandering another person. Use her as a peacemaker to stand up for what's right, showing the love of Jesus to everyone. Amen.

27

Submission to Authority

Let everyone be subject to the governing authorities, for there is no authority except that which God has established. The authorities that exist have been established by God.

ROMANS 13:1

LORD GOD,

Give my daughter strength to submit to leaders in her church, school, community, and nation. May she understand that limits and laws are in place for her safety and well-being. Help her to show self-control when tempted to drive recklessly, disrespect property, or insult authority. May she follow the rules out of obedience to You, trusting You are in control. Reward her with honor and peace. Amen.

28

A Willing Heart

Do everything without grumbling or arguing, so that you may become blameless and pure, "children of God without fault in a warped and crooked generation."

PHILIPPIANS 2:14-15

HEAVENLY FATHER,

I pray that my daughter would have a willing heart to follow wherever You lead. Give her strength to tackle challenging tasks and assignments without complaining. Let her help and serve others with a cheerful spirit. When she faces hard times, give her courage and endurance to make it through. May she obey You in all things with a pure heart, shining Your light in these dark days. Amen.

29

Wisdom with Her Words

A gossip betrays a confidence, but a trustworthy person keeps a secret.
PROVERBS 11:13

LORD,

Give my daughter wisdom with her words. Let her friends have confidence in her integrity and respect. Help her to resist temptation to share secrets and gossip. Give her discernment to recognize who she can trust with her personal life. Guard her from slander and gossip that can damage her reputation and ruin relationships. Bless her with an upright heart as You keep her secure in Your love. Amen.

30

Intimacy with God

"Do not fear, for I have redeemed you;
I have summoned you by name; you are Mine."
ISAIAH 43:1

FATHER GOD,
I confess that I am terrified my daughter will never know You. Replace my fear with trust, to believe that You will call her to Yourself. Claim her as Your own—may her name be written in heaven in the Book of Life. Give her ears to hear Your words of love, and eyes to see Your presence. Break down every barrier that is keeping her from running to You. Replace her doubts with faith that will last. Amen.

31

Freedom from Addiction

"I have the right to do anything," you say—but not everything is beneficial. "I have the right to do anything"—but I will not be mastered by anything.

1 CORINTHIANS 6:12

LORD,

It's tempting for my daughter to seek comfort in the pleasures of this world, rather than You. Keep her from dependence on food, sex, shopping, entertainment, drugs, relationships, alcohol—anything that falsely promises peace or happiness. Protect my daughter and set her free from any addiction that could ruin her life. Be her strength and her source of joy in every moment. Amen.

32

Direction for Her Life

Your word is a lamp for my feet, a light on my path.
PSALM 119:105

FATHER,

My daughter is at a crossroads; she doesn't know which way to go. Move her heart to desire Your perfect plan. Speak through Your Word so she knows which path to take. Help her to understand how Scripture applies to her life as she makes choices from day to day. Let her walk in Your light without stumbling in the darkness of this world. Give her faithful guidance for every step. Amen.

33

Her Image

Charm is deceptive, and beauty is fleeting; but a woman who fears the LORD is to be praised.

PROVERBS 31:30

RIGHTEOUS FATHER,

The world tells my daughter that her worth is found in her appearance. Guard her heart and mind from believing that beauty depends on perfect skin, hair and the size of her jeans. Give her peace when she's worried about looking just right. Let her please You instead of trying to live up to people's expectations. Fill her with Your beauty—perfect love that never ends. Amen.

34

How to Discipline Her

Discipline your children, and they will give you peace;
they will bring you the delights you desire.

PROVERBS 29:17

LORD,

Show me how to discipline my daughter with wisdom and love. Use the consequences of her actions to train her in obedience. Keep me from anger that seeks to punish rather than to help and guide. Make me courageous in holding to what's right, even if she argues and complains. Reward us with peace and joy as my daughter does what's right. Amen.

35

A Generous Heart

Each of you should give what you have decided in your heart to give, not reluctantly or under compulsion, for God loves a cheerful giver.

2 CORINTHIANS 9:7

LORD GOD,

You lavish Your love upon us—give Your heart of generosity to my daughter. Make her eager to share her blessings instead of hoarding Your gifts for herself. Let her share out of a pure heart, finding joy in giving to anyone in need. Guard her from selfishness that will keep her from loving others and shining Your light. Fill her with thanks for the good things that come from Your hand. Amen.

36

A Good Reputation

A good name is more desirable than great riches;
to be esteemed is better than silver or gold.
PROVERBS 22:1

FATHER,

Keep my daughter's reputation safely in Your hands. Protect her from slander and lies that would tear her down. Give her wisdom and self-control so that impulsive choices don't ruin her good name. Surround her with friends who walk in goodness and truth. Make her a young woman of honor, showing integrity in every situation. Let her be known for her character as she commits her way to You. Amen.

37

Strength When Suffering Persecution

"Blessed are you when people insult you, persecute you and falsely say all kinds of evil against you because of Me."
MATTHEW 5:11

HOLY LORD,

Living for You will make my daughter stand out in this world. Give her strength to hold firmly to her faith even if she walks alone. Encourage her heart when she's rejected, insulted, or harassed for following Jesus. Give her compassion for Your people who suffer abuse and even death as Christians. Protect her from fear and pour out blessings in her life when she suffers in Your name. Amen.

38

Her Training

Start children off on the way they should go, and even when they are old they will not turn from it.
PROVERBS 22:6

FATHER,

Give me wisdom in how to teach and train my daughter. Show me how to encourage her talents and develop the strengths of her personality. Let me guide her in the truth of Your Word as she grows. Allow our relationship to flourish so my love and influence remain a blessing in her life. Bring her to maturity, firmly established on the path You've laid out for her future. Thank You for the privilege of raising my precious daughter. Amen.

39

Being Bullied

"But I tell you, love your enemies and pray for those who persecute you, that you may be children of your Father in heaven."

MATTHEW 5:44-45

LORD,

You loved us first, when we were lost in our sins and didn't love You at all. I pray that my daughter would have Your heart, and love her enemies. Fill her with kindness and compassion when she's bullied or insulted. Teach her to pray for those who come against her—that they would turn to Jesus and find peace. Give her patience and courage to remain loving through it all. Amen.

40

True Beauty

Your beauty should not come from outward adornment, such as elaborate hairstyles and the wearing of gold jewelry or fine clothes. Rather, it should be that of your inner self, the unfading beauty of a gentle and quiet spirit, which is of great worth in God's sight.

1 PETER 3:3-4

RIGHTEOUS FATHER,

Guard my daughter from defining her beauty by what she sees in the mirror. Let her look past the outer display of fashion, hair, and makeup, and value what's in the heart. Help her to be gentle and quiet instead of showing off to get attention. Keep her from judging other girls by their appearance. Give her a peaceful, tender spirit that is lovely for all to see. Amen.

41

A Firm Faith in Jesus

See to it that no one takes you captive through hollow and deceptive philosophy, which depends on human tradition and the elemental spiritual forces of this world rather than on Christ.

COLOSSIANS 2:8

LORD JESUS,

The enemy and the world want to replace Your truth with lies. My daughter might hear that salvation is found in rituals or traditions instead of Jesus. She might be pressured to deny You as her authority and the Creator of the world. Protect her from believing anyone who would turn her away from You and Your Word. Guard her heart from doubt. Keep her secure in a faith that can't be shaken. Amen.

42

A Forgiving Heart

Do not repay evil with evil or insult with insult. On the contrary, repay evil with blessing, because to this you were called so that you may inherit a blessing.

1 PETER 3:9

LORD,

Any insult makes my daughter want to lash out with rudeness of her own. A push leads to a shove. Gossip stirs up more gossip. Move in my daughter's heart so she can love others instead of taking revenge. Let her show patience and forgiveness instead of fighting for her rights. May she receive Your blessings as she becomes a blessing to others. Amen.

43

Compassion like Jesus

Therefore, as God's chosen people, holy and dearly loved, clothe yourselves with compassion, kindness, humility, gentleness and patience.
COLOSSIANS 3:12

FATHER,

Give my daughter Your heart of compassion for everyone. Soften her heart for the hurting. Use her to care for the sick, the poor, and the outcast. Let her treat others as special and important. Help her to be gentle, even when she's treated harshly. Give her patience when she's provoked or treated unfairly. Bring Your kindness and love to the world through her life. Amen.

44

Doing Good

Let us not become weary in doing good, for at the proper time we will reap a harvest if we do not give up. Therefore, as we have opportunity, let us do good to all people, especially to those who belong to the family of believers.

GALATIANS 6:9-10

LORD,

Show my daughter how she can be a blessing in this world. Teach her to give to the poor, encourage the hurting, and help the weak. Open her eyes to see the ways she can share Your love. Give her strength to keep on giving and serving, even when she's tired or feels unappreciated. Let her discover Your beautiful rewards for doing good. Amen.

45

An Inquisitive Mind

Apply your heart to instruction and
your ears to words of knowledge.

PROVERBS 23:12

HOLY LORD,

Give my daughter an eager, inquisitive mind that loves to learn. Help her to value her education and commit to her studies. When the work is challenging, give her strength to finish well. Surround her with wise teachers who will encourage her along the way. Equip her to serve You with the skills and knowledge she receives. Guide her steps, fill her mind with truth, and reward her with wisdom and success. Amen.

46

Respecting Authority

Children, obey your parents in everything,
for this pleases the Lord.
COLOSSIANS 3:20

FATHER,

My daughter sometimes struggles to obey what I ask her to do. She can be disrespectful and resistant to my authority, keeping peace from our home. Help her to submit herself to Your design for family by honoring me as her parent. Give her a cheerful, humble attitude so she can listen and cooperate. Give me wisdom, love, and patience as she learns obedience. Let my daughter be pleasing to You. Amen.

47

Care for Animals

The righteous care for the needs of their animals,
but the kindest acts of the wicked are cruel.
PROVERBS 12:10

FATHER OF ALL,

Thank You for Your beautiful creation and the living creatures we enjoy. Give my daughter a compassionate heart that seeks to protect the animals You've made. Teach her to be diligent in caring for her pets. Let her stand up for weak and abandoned animals that have no defense. As she loves Your created world, let her tender heart be a witness of Your great love for everyone. Amen.

48

Standing Up for Others

My whole being will exclaim, "Who is like You, Lord?
You rescue the poor from those too strong for them,
the poor and needy from those who rob them."
PSALM 35:10

LORD GOD,

Your power and love are wonderful! You stand up for the weak and rescue us from trouble. Give Your heart of mercy to my daughter. Give her strength to stand up for those who can't defend themselves. Fill her hands with blessings so she can share with the poor and needy. Make her courageous to fight every kind of injustice and oppression—living out Your love and truth in this world. Amen.

49

Easing Her Anxiety

Anxiety weighs down the heart, but a kind word cheers it up.

PROVERBS 12:25

LORD,

My daughter can become paralyzed by stress and fear. She worries about her friendships, her grades, her safety, and her future. Doubts and insecurities steal her happiness. Let Your love and peace melt away her anxieties. Help her to trust You in every situation. Give her joy as she finds You faithful. Give me encouraging words to build her up and put a smile on her face. Amen.

50

Liberty from Depression

Why, my soul, are you downcast? Why so
disturbed within me? Put your hope in God,
for I will yet praise Him, my Savior and my God.
PSALM 42:5

FATHER,

My daughter doesn't always cope so well with her struggles. In times like these, depression steals her joy. Fill her with hope by Your Spirit. Give her faith to believe You will never leave her side. Let her trust in Your love, knowing You are everything she needs. Open her eyes to see Your goodness, and let her praise Your name as You lift her up. Amen.

51

Living in Unity

How good and pleasant it is when
God's people live together in unity!
PSALM 133:1

LORD GOD,

Conflict, competition, and criticism are spoiling the peace in our home. Fill my daughter with love so she'll work to get along with others. Help her to desire good things for everyone instead of having her own way. Let her show respect for people's ideas and opinions. Give her a forgiving spirit when she's offended. Enable my daughter to be a peacemaker, encourager, and helper to her family and friends each day. Amen.

52

Her Witness

In your hearts revere Christ as Lord. Always be prepared to give an answer to everyone who asks you to give the reason for the hope that you have.

1 PETER 3:15

HOLY FATHER,

I pray that my daughter would love You with all of her heart, her soul, and her strength. Fill her with hope, flowing out of the joy of knowing Jesus. Give her the words to say when she's asked to explain her trust in You. Keep her from any fear or embarrassment about sharing what You've done in her life. Use my daughter to shine the light of the gospel in this lost and hurting world. Amen.

53

God's Goodness

Children are a heritage from the Lord,
offspring a reward from Him.
PSALM 127:3

LORD JESUS,

Thank You for the gift of my daughter. You created her in Your image, and she's beautifully and wonderfully made. Help me to remember she was especially chosen for me and our family. Give me a heart that cherishes her as a reward from You. Knit us together in love, building a strong relationship that will last. May I always praise Your name for Your goodness to me—my daughter is a precious blessing from You. Amen.

54

God's Creation

Since the creation of the world God's invisible qualities—His eternal power and divine nature—have been clearly seen, being understood from what has been made, so that people are without excuse.

ROMANS 1:20

LORD,

Open my daughter's eyes to see how You're revealed in Your creation. Let the beauty and majesty of nature touch her heart and move her to worship You. Use her studies and knowledge of the natural world to confirm that You are the Creator of all things. Build her faith in You, our invisible God, through this marvelous universe You've made. Amen.

55

Changing a Critical Nature

"How can you say to your brother, 'Brother, let me take the speck out of your eye,' when you yourself fail to see the plank in your own eye? You hypocrite, first take the plank out of your eye, and then you will see clearly to remove the speck from your brother's eye."

LUKE 6:42

HOLY LORD,

My daughter can sometimes be quick to point out the mistakes and weaknesses of others. Give her a humble heart to see how she needs to grow and change before she criticizes people around her. Give her patience and mercy by Your Spirit. Let her long for goodness and obedience, to become more like Jesus every day. Inspire others to follow You by the love she displays in her life. Amen.

56

A Heart of Compassion

"To you who are listening I say: Love your enemies, do good to those who hate you, bless those who curse you, pray for those who mistreat you."

LUKE 6:27-28

HEAVENLY FATHER,

My daughter feels angry and hurt when she's rejected, teased, or insulted. She builds a wall around her heart and pulls away from others. She tends to hold on to grudges and refuses to give second chances. Help her to show compassion and to forgive. Let her show kindness by blessing and praying for her enemies. Through Jesus' love and strength, may she give grace and pursue peace with everyone in her life. Amen.

57

Knowing Jesus' Voice

"My sheep listen to My voice; I know them, and they follow Me. I give them eternal life, and they shall never perish; no one will snatch them out of My hand."

JOHN 10:27-28

FATHER,

Teach my daughter to recognize Your voice. Let her hear You when she prays and reads Your Word. Even when the world tries to drown You out, let her respond to Your call and follow You every day. Help her to trust that You will never let her go. As she suffers through any kind of struggle or temptation, let her know she's Yours as You hold her securely in Your hand. Amen.

58

Peace & Reconciliation

"If you are offering your gift at the altar and there remember that your brother or sister has something against you, leave your gift there in front of the altar. First go and be reconciled to them; then come and offer your gift."

MATTHEW 5:23-24

LORD GOD,

My daughter isn't perfect—she will make mistakes and let people down. She'll hurt others with her words and actions. Give her a loving heart that craves peace and reconciliation. Let her admit when she's wrong and seek forgiveness. Supply her with strength to make amends and rebuild broken relationships. Bless her with peace by Your Spirit. Amen.

59

Right Living

Let us behave decently, as in the daytime, not in carousing and drunkenness, not in sexual immorality and debauchery, not in dissension and jealousy. Rather, clothe yourselves with the Lord Jesus Christ, and do not think about how to gratify the desires of the flesh.

ROMANS 13:13-14

FATHER GOD,

My daughter will, at times, be tempted to seek happiness in partying, sexual experiences, and material possessions. Give her strength to resist the traps of drugs and alcohol. Guard her innocence. Give her wisdom in knowing where to look for fun and adventure. Fill her with gratitude for what You've given her, so she doesn't depend on money or "things" to satisfy. Let her life be conformed to the holiness of Jesus. Amen.

60

Confession & Prayer

Confess your sins to each other and pray for each other so that you may be healed. The prayer of a righteous person is powerful and effective.

JAMES 5:16

LORD,

Give my daughter a sensitive conscience that grieves when she disobeys You. Show her how freedom and blessings come through sharing her weaknesses with others. Provide godly people to pray for her and build her up. Give me wisdom as her parent, faithfully praying and helping her overcome her sins. Move through our prayers to bring Your healing and power into her life. Amen.

61

Protection from a Cruel World

Keep me safe from the traps set by evildoers, from the snares they have laid for me. Let the wicked fall into their own nets, while I pass by in safety.

PSALM 141:9-10

FATHER,

Guard my daughter from any schemes to do her harm or make her stumble. Protect her from online predators who would exploit her innocence. Keep her safe from bullying, damaging lies, and cruelty. Deliver her from destructive influences that tempt her to disobey Your Word. Surround her with Your angels everywhere she goes, that no evil person may touch her. Amen.

62

Training Her in Goodness

A rod and a reprimand impart wisdom,
but a child left undisciplined disgraces its mother.
PROVERBS 29:15

FATHER,

Teach me how to discipline my daughter as she grows. Show me how to train her in goodness and godliness. Give me wisdom in using rewards and consequences to shape her choices. When I'm weary of the work of parenting, build me up with strength to keep on teaching my child. Let my discipline bear fruit in her life, that she may live in obedience to You. Amen.

63

Resisting Peer Pressure

Am I now trying to win the approval of human beings, or of God? Or am I trying to please people? If I were still trying to please people, I would not be a servant of Christ.

GALATIANS 1:10

LORD,

There may be times when my daughter might be tempted to betray her conscience to fit in with the crowd. She could feel pressure to conform to the world's definition of what's fun, attractive, and true. Give my daughter courage to live as a servant of Christ. Make it her heart's desire to please You in everything, instead of trying to live up to people's expectations. Set her free to live in joyful obedience to You. Amen.

64

Her Gifts

If your gift is prophesying, then prophesy in accordance with your faith; if it is serving, then serve; if it is teaching, then teach; if it is to encourage, then give encouragement; if it is giving, then give generously; if it is to lead, do it diligently; if it is to show mercy, do it cheerfully.

ROMANS 12:6-8

FATHER,

Thank You for equipping us with strengths and abilities through the power of Your Spirit. Give my daughter wisdom to recognize how she can serve Your people and bless the world for Jesus. Fill her with joy when she helps, shares, teaches, or builds up others who are in need of Your love. May she depend on You to provide all she needs to do Your work, for Your glory. Amen.

65

Her Dreams

Hope deferred makes the heart sick,
but a longing fulfilled is a tree of life.
PROVERBS 13:12

LORD GOD,
My daughter is waiting for her dreams to come true. It's a struggle to have patience and believe that good things will come in Your perfect timing. Encourage her heart by Your love. Shape the desires and hopes of her heart so that she will seek Your perfect will. Give her faith to believe that You are always good and faithful. Amen.

66

Restoring Hope & Strength

Praise the Lord, my soul, and forget not all His benefits—who forgives all your sins and heals all your diseases, who redeems your life from the pit and crowns you with love and compassion.

PSALM 103:2-4

FATHER,

In this broken world, my daughter's heart will be wounded and her body will suffer sickness and injury. Hold her tenderly and bring Your comfort in the pain. Restore her hope and strength. Let her discover Your perfect love that heals as she cries out to You. Give her endurance to wait patiently for You as her great Physician. Amen.

67

Faith like a Child

Jesus called the children to Him and said, "Let the little children come to Me, and do not hinder them, for the kingdom of God belongs to such as these."

LUKE 18:16

FATHER GOD,

Thank You for cherishing my daughter, allowing her to love You and to know Your name. Give her a desire to come to You and worship. Tear down any barrier that would keep her from You. Never allow any person to discourage her from seeking Your face. Build up an unshakable faith in her young heart so that she will trust in You forever. Amen.

68

Appreciating What She Has

Then Jesus said to them, "Watch out! Be on your guard against all kinds of greed; life does not consist in an abundance of possessions."
LUKE 12:15

RIGHTEOUS LORD,
Nothing will destroy my daughter's joy and gratitude like a greedy heart. Fill her with appreciation for all You've done in her life. Open her eyes to see Your blessings, and the contentment to be fully satisfied. Guard her heart from loving Your gifts above You, the Giver. Let her discover true happiness in You as her loving Father. Amen.

69

Wisdom from God

If any of you lacks wisdom, you should ask God, who gives generously to all without finding fault, and it will be given to you.

JAMES 1:5

LORD,

My daughter needs Your direction as she makes choices in life. Help her to know which way to go as she makes plans for her education, career, and relationships. Give her a heart that seeks Your will, wanting to please You above herself. Let her trust Your guidance when she's confused or in doubt about the next steps to take. Amen.

70

Knowing God's Love

And I pray that you, being rooted and established in love, may have power, together with all the Lord's holy people, to grasp how wide and long and high and deep is the love of Christ, and to know this love that surpasses knowledge—that you may be filled to the measure of all the fullness of God.

EPHESIANS 3:17-19

HOLY FATHER,

When trials come or the evil in this world seems overwhelming, my daughter may doubt that You're really in control. She may wonder if Your light will overcome the darkness. Give her the power to comprehend that Your love is greater than we can imagine. Fill her to overflowing with the fullness of God. Overwhelm her life and her spirit with Your limitless love. Amen.

71

Deliverance from Temptation

If you think you are standing firm, be careful that you don't fall! No temptation has overtaken you except what is common to mankind. And God is faithful; He will not let you be tempted beyond what you can bear. But when you are tempted, He will also provide a way out so that you can endure it.

1 CORINTHIANS 10:12-13

LORD,

Keep my daughter from overconfidence in her young faith, thinking she'll never fall. Draw her close so she'll depend on Your strength to stand firm. Give her wisdom to recognize the enemy's schemes. Deliver her from any temptation that will keep her from living in obedience to You. Amen.

72

A Pure Heart & Mind

Flee the evil desires of youth and pursue righteousness, faith, love and peace, along with those who call on the Lord out of a pure heart.

2 TIMOTHY 2:22

FATHER,

Fill my daughter with longing for You. Let her seek stronger faith, greater obedience, and deeper love as she grows. Guard her heart from pride, lust, and selfishness that will drive her away from You. Surround her with encouragement and help in following You so she can find peace that only You supply. Let her remain pure of heart and mind as she discovers Your love that never fails. Amen.

73

Keeping Her Safe

The LORD will keep you from all harm—He will watch over your life; the LORD will watch over your coming and going both now and forevermore.

PSALM 121:7-8

LORD GOD,

Thank You for Your constant watch over my daughter. She is never out of Your reach, never out of Your sight, and never too far for You to bring her home. Continue to protect her by Your love and power. Surround her with angels and shield her from the evil one. Guide her steps and let her cling to You as her loving Father. Keep her under Your wing forever. Amen.

74

Having Hope

May the God of hope fill you with all joy and peace
as you trust in Him, so that you may overflow
with hope by the power of the Holy Spirit.

ROMANS 15:13

LORD JESUS,

You are the One who can calm any storm in my daughter's life. No matter the difficulty or uncertainty, help my daughter to trust in You. Replace her worries with peace and her discouragement with hope. Fill her with Your Spirit so her faith will rise above any fear. Thank You for the joy that You give, even in the darkest days. Amen.

75

Living in Peace

The entire law is fulfilled in keeping this one command: "Love your neighbor as yourself." If you bite and devour each other, watch out or you will be destroyed by each other.

GALATIANS 5:14-15

FATHER,

My daughter can at times be consumed by her own needs and desires, caring for herself above anyone else. Give her joy in loving others. Keep her from selfishness that competes for attention and blessings. Grow kindness and generosity in her heart so she can live in peace with everyone. Transform her mind and spirit with gratitude and trust in You. Amen.

76

Teach Her Self-Control

Now you must also rid yourselves of all such things as these: anger, rage, malice, slander, and filthy language from your lips.

COLOSSIANS 3:8

LORD,

It's tempting for my daughter to lash out when she's angry. When she gives way to her temper, she hurts even the ones she loves. Teach my daughter self-control so she's not ruled by her emotions. Guard her lips from hateful, ugly words and keep her from destructive behavior. Replace her rage with forgiveness and peace. Transform her heart so she's known for her patience and love. Amen.

77

When She Wanders

"What do you think? If a man owns a hundred sheep, and one of them wanders away, will he not leave the ninety-nine on the hills and go to look for the one that wandered off?"

MATTHEW 18:12

FATHER,

The distractions of this world could easily cause my daughter's faith in You to falter. She could be tempted to live for herself instead of Jesus. The enemy's lies could persuade her to doubt Your Word. I know she is precious to You—pursue her heart and draw her close to Yourself. Rescue her from sin, strengthen her belief in Your truth, and let her know Your love. Amen.

78

Her Passions

Do not love the world or anything in the world. If anyone loves the world, love for the Father is not in them. For everything in the world—the lust of the flesh, the lust of the eyes, and the pride of life—comes not from the Father but from the world.

1 JOHN 2:15-16

LORD GOD,

The world competes for my daughter's heart and mind. It tantalizes her with pleasure, possessions, and pride that will only turn her away from You. Give her wisdom to see that the world's form of happiness is an illusion—true joy is only found in You. Fill her with Your love and a faith that can't be shaken. Be her greatest desire. Amen.

79

Speaking Up for Others

Speak up for those who cannot speak for themselves, for the rights of all who are destitute. Speak up and judge fairly; defend the rights of the poor and needy.

PROVERBS 31:8-9

HEAVENLY FATHER,

Thank You for Your justice that guards the rights of the weak and the poor. Give my daughter a courageous spirit to speak up for those who can't defend themselves. Use her to relieve suffering and restore dignity. Fill her with mercy and compassion for all people. Like Jesus, may she love the unlovable and remember the forgotten. Bless her for standing for the truth. Amen.

80

Courage in Times of Trouble

"The Lord Himself goes before you and will be with you; He will never leave you nor forsake you. Do not be afraid; do not be discouraged."
DEUTERONOMY 31:8

FATHER,

My daughter is scared to face the changes and challenges before her. Fear is suppressing excitement and hope for the future. Inspire her with confidence that You'll never leave her side. Help her to trust that You're in control and have wonderful plans in store for her life. Give her courage to follow wherever You may lead, knowing she'll never walk alone. Amen.

81

Letting Go of Anger

"In your anger do not sin": Do not let the sun go down while you are still angry, and do not give the devil a foothold.

EPHESIANS 4:26-27

LORD,

My daughter is sometimes tempted to hold on to anger and resentment toward others. She can refuse to let go of the past and to forgive. By Your Spirit, please replace the bitterness with love. Keep the enemy from hardening her heart. Help her to always lay down the grudge she's carrying. Set her free from anger today to live in peace tomorrow. Amen.

82

Spiritual Growth

Like newborn babies, crave pure spiritual milk,
so that by it you may grow up in your salvation,
now that you have tasted that the Lord is good.
1 PETER 2:2-3

FATHER,

My daughter's faith needs nourishment to grow. Give her a hunger for Your Word, so she can grow in Your truth. Let her taste and see how good You are. May she seek Your face in prayer and learn to recognize Your voice. Surround her with other believers to teach, pray, and encourage my child to follow You. Enable me to live in faithful obedience as an example in her life. Amen.

83

A Respectful Attitude

Have confidence in your leaders and submit to their authority, because they keep watch over you as those who must give an account. Do this so that their work will be a joy, not a burden, for that would be of no benefit to you.

HEBREWS 13:17

LORD,

Thank You for placing authorities over my daughter's life to teach, serve, and protect her from harm. Help her to appreciate the time and energy their positions demand. Humble her heart to submit to her leaders' rules and instruction, trusting they're for her good. Make her a blessing by her respectful attitude. Reward her obedience with Your love. Amen.

84

Sexual Purity

Flee from sexual immorality. All other sins a person commits are outside the body, but whoever sins sexually, sins against their own body.

1 CORINTHIANS 6:18

LORD GOD,

In this world that distorts the beauty of sexual intimacy, keep my daughter pure in body and mind. Protect her innocence and give her the strength to turn away from any kind of immorality. Give her wisdom to understand that her husband's love is worth waiting for. Devote her heart to You so she can live in pure obedience to Your Word. Amen.

85

Encouragement & Strength

Praise be to the God and Father of our Lord Jesus Christ, the Father of compassion and the God of all comfort, who comforts us in all our troubles, so that we can comfort those in any trouble with the comfort we ourselves receive from God.

2 CORINTHIANS 1:3-4

HOLY LORD,

My daughter is tired and troubled. Embrace her with love—may she know You as her comfort, help, and strength. Use the difficulties she suffers to create compassion for others going through hard times. Let her share the encouragement she receives from You, becoming a blessing as she is blessed. Thank You for Your love that never fails. Amen.

86

Loving Others

"If you love those who love you, what reward will you get? Are not even the tax collectors doing that? And if you greet only your own people, what are you doing more than others? Do not even pagans do that?"

MATTHEW 5:46-47

FATHER,

Give my daughter a loving heart for everyone, even if they don't love her in return. Lift her eyes to see past her own circle of friends. Give her courage to reach out to others. Fill her with compassion for the unpopular, the unwelcome, and the unlovely. Use my daughter's kindness and respect to shine the light of Jesus wherever she goes. Amen.

87

A Teachable Heart

The way of fools seems right to them,
but the wise listen to advice.
PROVERBS 12:15

LORD,

My daughter has choices—to be wise or foolish, humble or proud, yielding or stubborn. Give her a teachable heart that welcomes advice. Help her to understand the limits of her experience and knowledge. Protect her from having to learn the hard way, by trying to figure out life on her own. Build up our relationship so my influence can help her along the way. Amen.

88

Finding True Happiness

I know what it is to be in need, and I know what it is to have plenty. I have learned the secret of being content in any and every situation, whether well fed or hungry, whether living in plenty or in want.

PHILIPPIANS 4:12

HEAVENLY FATHER,

It's tempting for my daughter to depend on "stuff" to feel happy and secure. She becomes obsessed about what she'd like to buy, and she pressures me to make every wish come true. Teach her the secret of being content. Set her free in knowing she can find joy, no matter what she's gained or lost. Give her gratitude for all the ways You pour love into her life. Amen.

89

Godly Role Models

Remember your leaders, who spoke the word of God to you.
Consider the outcome of their way of life and imitate their faith.
Jesus Christ is the same yesterday and today and forever.
Do not be carried away by all kinds of strange teachings.

HEBREWS 13:7-9

LORD,

My daughter needs good judgment in choosing her role models. Surround my daughter with spiritual examples who will show the way in following You. Give her eyes to see their obedience, purity, and wisdom as they live for Jesus. Protect her from anyone who would turn her away from Your Word. Let my own faith and love for You be worth imitating as I lead my child. Amen.

90

Her Future Husband

Husbands, love your wives, just as Christ loved
the church and gave Himself up for her.
EPHESIANS 5:25

HOLY LORD,

In Your perfect plans for the future, provide a loving husband for my daughter. Let him be fully devoted to You and Your Word. Prepare him even now to serve and protect his family. Give him a heart like Jesus so he can surrender his pride and selfish desires. Fill him with Your love that will overflow into his home. Bless him as he cherishes my daughter. Amen.

91

Focusing Her Thoughts on God

Finally, brothers and sisters, whatever is true, whatever is noble, whatever is right, whatever is pure, whatever is lovely, whatever is admirable—if anything is excellent or praiseworthy—think about such things.

PHILIPPIANS 4:8

FATHER,

Transform my daughter's mind by Your Spirit. Protect her from lies and confusion by the knowledge of Your truth. Let her dream of pleasing You with her goals and plans. Give her a grace-filled perspective to see the good in other people. Help her to discern between what's pure and sinful, noble and corrupt, beautiful and broken. Captivate my daughter's thoughts with Jesus. Amen.

92

Speaking Words of Blessing

Do not let any unwholesome talk come out of your mouths, but only what is helpful for building others up according to their needs, that it may benefit those who listen.

EPHESIANS 4:29

FATHER GOD,

Teach my daughter to understand the power of her words. Let her speak words of blessing instead of tearing others down. Guard her lips from profanity, gossip, lies, and slander. Give her wisdom to know when to speak and when to stay silent. Help her to bring love, encouragement, and truth to every conversation. Fill her mouth with truth and praise to Your name. Amen.

93

Confessing Secret Sins

Then I acknowledged my sin to You and did not cover up my iniquity. I said, "I will confess my transgressions to the Lord." And You forgave the guilt of my sin.

PSALM 32:5

LORD,

Whenever my daughter sins, embarrassment, stubbornness, and shame often keep her from confessing her sins to You. Encourage her heart to trust in Your mercy. Let her discover the freedom and peace that come from bringing her guilt to You. Give her a joyful heart as she receives Your forgiveness and love. Thank You for Your mercy and grace in her life. Amen.

94

Overcoming Her Doubts

Yet he did not waver through unbelief regarding the promise of God, but was strengthened in his faith and gave glory to God, being fully persuaded that God had power to do what He had promised.

ROMANS 4:20-21

FATHER,

Help my daughter to believe Your promises—that Jesus is alive and coming again, that Your love never fails, and that Your Word is forever true. The world will assault her faith and the enemy will try to steal her hope. Help her to stand firm so she can trust You without wavering. Overcome her doubts and help her to keep her eyes on You. Let her see Your power, and praise You forever. Amen.

95

Her Church Family

Let us consider how we may spur one another on toward love and good deeds, not giving up meeting together, as some are in the habit of doing, but encouraging one another—and all the more as you see the Day approaching.

HEBREWS 10:24-25

LORD JESUS,

In these dark days, my daughter needs the encouragement of God's people. Fill her with love for Your church. Use other believers to set an example of love and holiness for my child. Let her find a place to belong in Your spiritual family, so she never has to walk this life alone. Make us faithful to each other until You come and take us home. Amen.

96

Staying on the Path of Purity

How can a young person stay on the path of purity? By living according to Your word. I seek You with all my heart; do not let me stray from Your commands.

PSALM 119:9-10

FATHER,

My daughter can receive mixed messages about who she is and how she's supposed to live. Clear up the confusion by giving her a love for Your Word. Deepen her understanding of the Scriptures. Let her find direction, wisdom, and truth as she seeks You. Keep her feet on the path of purity as she obeys You in every way. Capture her heart and hold her close. Amen.

97

Being an Example for Others

Don't let anyone look down on you because you are young, but set an example for the believers in speech, in conduct, in love, in faith and in purity.

1 TIMOTHY 4:12

LORD,

Thank You that my daughter can know You, growing in faith and wisdom even as a child. Let her speak words of truth and love like Jesus. Give her an excellent reputation as she obeys Your Word. Keep her faithful and pure as she faces the challenges of growing up. Use her life as an example to everyone as she loves You more and more. Amen.

98

Choosing the Right Friends

The righteous choose their friends carefully,
but the way of the wicked leads them astray.
PROVERBS 12:26

LORD GOD,
Give my daughter wisdom to choose the right friends who will build her up and bring her closer to You. Set her free from the traps of popularity and pressure to conform. Protect her from anyone who would wound her spirit and discourage her faith. Provide her with friends who love You as their Savior. Thank You for being the best Friend she'll ever know. Amen.

99

Her Needs

My God will meet all your needs according to
the riches of His glory in Christ Jesus.

PHILIPPIANS 4:19

FATHER,

You know everything that my daughter needs for health, knowledge, and security. Help her to trust You in every situation because You care for her. Let her bring every concern to You in prayer, and out of Your riches give more than she could hope for. Build her faith and hope in Your amazing love as You provide. Thank You for holding her life in Your hands. Amen.

100

Her Source of Rest

"Come to Me, all you who are weary and burdened, and I will give you rest. Take My yoke upon you and learn from Me, for I am gentle and humble in heart, and you will find rest for your souls. For My yoke is easy and My burden is light."
MATTHEW 11:28-30

HEAVENLY FATHER,

My daughter is exhausted from striving to become all she hopes to be. She chases beauty, success, and perfection. Release her from the pressure. Let her receive the love and mercy that You so freely give. Help her to put her life in Your hands, letting You lead the way. Be her source of love and righteousness as she puts her trust in You. Amen.

101

Dependence on God

"Remain in Me, as I also remain in you. No branch can bear fruit by itself; it must remain in the vine. Neither can you bear fruit unless you remain in Me. I am the vine; you are the branches. If you remain in Me and I in you, you will bear much fruit; apart from Me you can do nothing."

JOHN 15:4-5

LORD GOD,

Teach my daughter to depend on You for everything. Let her lean on Your strength to obey, and Your Word for the truth. Save her from pride in her own goodness and accomplishments. Draw her close and keep her faithful. Keep her from forgetting You and making her way alone. Let the fruit of love and righteousness be borne in her life as she remains in You. Amen.